KID CHEFS

COOKING WITH COCOA

Rose Miles

Enslow PUBLISHING

Please visit our website, www.enslow.com. For a free color catalog of all our high-quality books,
call toll free 1-800-398-2504 or fax 1-877-980-4454

Published in 2027 by
Enslow Publishing
2544 Clinton Street
Buffalo, NY 14224

Portions of this work were originally authored by Kristen Rajczak and published as *Ingredients for a Healthy Life: Creative Cocoa Recipes*. All new material in this edition is authored by Rose Miles.

Cataloging-in-Publication Data
Names: Miles, Rose.
Title: Cooking with cocoa / Rose Miles.
Description: Buffalo, NY : Enslow Publishing, 2027. | Series: Kid chefs | Includes glossary and index.
Identifiers: ISBN 9781978548480 (pbk.) | ISBN 9781978548497 (library bound) | ISBN 9781978548503 (ebook)
Subjects: LCSH: Cooking (Chocolate)--Juvenile literature. | Chocolate--Juvenile literature. | Chocolate processing--Juvenile literature. | Cacao--Juvenile literature.
Classification: LCC TX767.C5 M674 2027 | DDC 641.3374--dc23

Printed in China

Photos Credits: Cover, p. 1 Eivaisla/Shutterstock.com; cover, p. 1 Africa Studio/Shutterstock.com; cover, p. 1 Nubes Studio/Shutterstock.com; cover, p. 1 Peter Hermes Furian/Shutterstock.com; cover, p. 1 Chiociolla/Shutterstock.com; p. 4, 6, 8, 10, 12, 15, 16, 18, 20 ricorico/Shutterstock.com; p. 5 Kabachki.photo/Shutterstock.com; p. 6 Valentyn Volkov/Shutterstock.com; p. 7 Ibrahim_Lutra/Shutterstock.com; p. 9 Anthony Schreier/Shutterstock.com; p. 10 MaraZe/Shutterstock.com; p. 11 Spalnic/Shutterstock.com; p. 13 parveez123/Shutterstock.com; p. 15 New Africa/Shutterstock.com; p. 16 Nataly Studio/Shutterstock.com; p. 17 Photoongraphy/Shutterstock.com; p. 18 Robbie M/Shutterstock.com; p. 19 Moiz 8009/Shutterstock.com; p. 20 Maha Arts/Shutterstock.com; p. 21 Pixel-Shot/Shutterstock.com; p. 22 Maks Peoplenko/Shutterstock.com

CPSIA compliance information: Batch #QSENS27: For further information, contact Enslow Publishing, New York, New York, at 1-800-398-2504.

Contents

Recipes in this book may use knives, mixers, and hot stove tops. Ask for an adult's help when using these tools.

Words in the glossary appear in **bold** type the first time they are used in the text.

For the Chocolate Lovers

Chocolate! This tasty treat is the best-known product created from the cocoa bean. From cakes and brownies to pudding and hot fudge, cocoa is part of some very tasty desserts. But did you know that cocoa isn't actually sweet? The sweetness many people love is due to the sugar that's included in many dessert **recipes**.

By itself, cocoa is good for your body. Keep reading to learn more about this useful **ingredient**. You'll also find ways to use cocoa in any meal. You might just find your new favorite recipe!

Do You Have Allergies?

The recipes in this book may use ingredients that contain or have come into contact with nuts, gluten, dairy products, and other common causes of **allergies**. If you have any food allergies, please ask a parent or teacher for help when cooking and tasting!

Adding cocoa to your favorite recipes can be healthy and tasty too!

Cacao Trees

Chocolate bars don't grow on trees! But cocoa beans do, which is where chocolate comes from. Cocoa beans are the seeds of the cacao (kuh-KOW) tree. They're found inside long yellow fruit pods that look a bit like cucumbers. The pods grow on the trunk and branches of the tree. Inside a cocoa bean's hard shell is a little kernel called the nib. The nib is what's used to make cocoa products.

Cacao trees were first grown in South and Central America. Today, they're found in parts of Africa and Asia as well. They are commonly grown on small farms within 20 degrees of the **equator**.

Tasty Tidbits

People around the world enjoy the products made from more than 4.4 million tons (4 million mt) of cocoa beans each year.

The cacao tree is an evergreen tree with shiny leaves that start red and turn green.

From Central America to Europe

People have been eating cacao beans for a long time. The Maya, Toltec, and Aztec peoples of Central America were the first to use the fruit of the cacao tree more than 3,000 years ago! When the Spanish explorers arrived in the 1500s, the Aztecs taught them to make a tasty cocoa drink.

Spanish explorers brought cocoa beans back to Spain. The Spanish kept these flavorful beans a secret for almost 100 years! But in the 1600s, cocoa drinks became popular across Europe. “Chocolate houses” selling hot cocoa popped up in cities like London, England, during the 1700s.

Tasty Tidbits

In 1876, a man in Switzerland made the first milk chocolate. Daniel Peter had experimented for eight years before finding the perfect formula.

Simple Chicken Mole

makes 4 servings

Ingredients:

1 ½ pounds chicken, cut into cubes or strips
4 tablespoons olive oil, divided
1 teaspoon cayenne pepper
½ teaspoon black pepper
2 tablespoons chili powder
2 teaspoons cumin
1 teaspoon cinnamon
1 ½ ounces unsweetened chocolate
4 (14.5-ounce) cans stewed tomatoes

*Mole (MOH-lay) is a sauce often used in Mexican **cuisine**. Making a traditional mole usually takes a lot of time and many ingredients. This recipe makes it a little simpler!*

Directions:

1. Mix together black pepper and cayenne pepper in a bowl. Add chicken and toss until it's coated.
2. Heat 2 tablespoons of olive oil in a large pot on the stove top and add the chicken. Cook until the chicken is done, with no pink at its center. Remove chicken with a slotted spoon and set it aside.
3. In a bowl, mix chili powder, cumin, and cinnamon.
4. Heat 2 tablespoons of olive oil in the same pot and add the chili powder mix. Stir the spices and oil with a spoon for about 6 minutes, or until the mixture is blackened and hot.
5. Lower the stove top's heat. Add the chocolate, and stir until it's melted. Add the stewed tomatoes and bring the mixture to a boil. Stir well.
6. After about 10 minutes, put the chicken back in the pot. Continue cooking until heated through, about 5 minutes. Serve warm.

Heart Healthy

Cocoa became popular across Europe. It was known as a "health-giving" food among the wealthy. Today, scientists have found this to be true!

Cocoa powder has a high amount of **antioxidants**. It may keep your heart healthier by helping you maintain lower blood pressure. Cocoa contains healthy **fats** and has been said to lower the risk of some illnesses.

However, when cocoa is mixed with lots of sugar, its **nutritional value** is less. Chocolate cookies and brownies can still be enjoyed, but just a little at a time!

Tasty Tidbits

Using cocoa powder and eating small amounts of dark chocolate are the best ways to gain cocoa's health benefits.

Cocoa Granola

makes about 12 cups of cereal

Ingredients:

8 cups quick-cooking oats
1 cup sliced toasted almonds
2 cups unsweetened coconut
½ cup light butter
¾ cup real maple syrup
¼ cup unsweetened cocoa powder
½ tablespoon vanilla extract

Directions:

1. Preheat the oven to 250 degrees.
2. Combine oats, almonds, and coconut in a large bowl. Stir together.
3. Melt butter in a small measuring cup. Add the maple syrup and cocoa powder. Stir together and microwave for about 30 seconds, or until the mixture is smooth. Add the vanilla.
4. Pour the maple syrup mixture over the bowl of oats, almonds, and coconut. Stir so the dry ingredients are coated.
5. Spread the mixture onto two cookie sheets. Bake at 250 degrees for 30 minutes. Use a spatula to turn the granola, then bake for another 30 minutes, or until golden brown.
6. Allow to cool. Store in an airtight container.

Make this easy recipe for a healthy—and chocolaty—breakfast! It can be eaten on its own or as a topping for yogurt.

How Cocoa Beans Become Chocolate

Cocoa beans must be **processed** before they become cocoa powder or chocolate. First, the fruit of the cacao tree is picked and the beans removed. Then, the beans are put into leaf-lined holes in the ground or shallow boxes for about a week to lose water and **ferment**.

The beans are dried and roasted. The nibs are then ground to release the fat in them—cocoa butter—and form a paste called chocolate liquor, or cocoa mass. Cocoa butter might be pressed out to make cocoa powder, or more cocoa butter may be added to make chocolate candy. To make chocolate, sugar and sometimes milk or other flavors are added to the chocolate liquor.

Tasty Tidbits

Beyond the basic process, different places have their own way of making chocolate. Belgian chocolate makers, for example, receive the main chocolate-making ingredient as a liquid in a tank on a truck, while many others have it delivered in solid form.

The Best Chocolate Chip Cookies

Ingredients:

2 ¼ cups flour
1 teaspoon baking soda
¼ teaspoon salt
¾ cup brown sugar
½ cup white sugar
½ cup light butter
1 teaspoon vanilla extract
2 egg whites
¾ cup chocolate chips

You'll see lots of different types of chocolate chips in the grocery store, such as dark chocolate, milk chocolate, and semi-sweet chocolate. Use whichever is your favorite!

Directions:

1. Preheat oven to 350 degrees. Line cookie sheets with parchment paper.
2. Combine flour, baking soda, and salt in a bowl. Mix together with a fork or whisk.
3. Microwave butter until just soft, about 15 to 30 seconds. Add it to a large bowl with both kinds of sugar. Mix well.
4. Separate your eggs. Then, add the whites to the butter and sugar mixture. Mix in the vanilla too.
5. A little at a time, blend in the flour mixture until the batter is smooth.
6. Mix in the chocolate chips.
7. Use a spoon to scoop the batter onto the cookie sheets, leaving a couple of inches between each one.
8. Bake for 10 minutes, or until lightly browned.
9. Allow cookies to cool for 2 minutes before removing from the sheet.
10. Repeat with remaining batter.

Chocolate and More Chocolate!

There are lots of kinds of chocolate. But what makes them different from each other?

Unsweetened baking chocolate is often used for baking. It is pure chocolate liquor with no sugar added, so it tastes bitter.

Milk chocolate actually has milk in it! Cocoa butter and chocolate liquor make up the base. Milk chocolate has sugar in it too. It is used in many types of candy bars. It is the most popular type of chocolate in the world!

Dark chocolate is less sweet than milk chocolate, though it does contain sugar and vanilla. What sets dark chocolate apart is the high cocoa content. It's usually about 30 to 80 percent cocoa! Dark chocolate has many health benefits because of the high cocoa content.

Peanut Butter Chocolate Frosting

makes about 1/2 cup

Ingredients:

¼ cup peanut butter
4 teaspoons pure maple syrup
2 tablespoons cocoa powder
4 teaspoons milk (or a bit more if you want a thinner result)
¾ teaspoon pure vanilla extract

Directions:

1. Use a fork to mix all the ingredients together.
2. Chill in a covered bowl in the fridge until you want to use it.

Chocolate and peanut butter are a yummy combination in this simple frosting recipe. If anyone in your family has a peanut allergy, you could try using sunflower seed butter or almond butter instead!

Tasty Tidbits

Is it chocolate if there's no cocoa in it? White chocolate is made of cocoa butter but not the cocoa solids in chocolate liquor, so it tastes like vanilla or other flavors it might be made with.

Mix It In

Did you know you can melt chocolate and make your own candy?

First, place the chocolate in a microwave-safe bowl. Then, microwave it for about 30 seconds at a time and stir. When it's smooth, mix in your favorite chocolate pairings, such as raisins or other dried fruit, nuts, coconut flakes, or even cereal!

Finally, spread the melted chocolate on a cookie sheet and pop it in the freezer. Once it's solid, break it into pieces for some yummy homemade chocolate candy!

Tasty Tidbits

The chocolate made for candy coating often has vegetable oil in it instead of cocoa butter to make it melt more easily. However, it often won't have as strong a chocolate flavor.

Homemade Hot Cocoa

makes 4 servings

Ingredients:

4 cups milk
4 tablespoons unsweetened cocoa
4 tablespoons honey
cinnamon (optional)

Skip those store-bought packets! Ask an adult for help using the stove top to make some great hot cocoa to share.

Directions:

1. Measure milk into a medium pan and place on the stove top.
2. Heat the milk on low until it just starts to boil.
3. Add the cocoa and honey to the milk. Mix until they are well combined.
4. Pour into mugs. Sprinkle cinnamon on top for added flavor!

Sweet and Savory

When you think of chocolate, you probably think about desserts. But cocoa can add a special flavor to any meal of the day!

Cocoa's flavor pairs well with many spices, such as cinnamon and chili pepper. It's often in spice rubs for meats like pork.

Have you ever seen pasta with a **savory** chocolate sauce? Or a chocolate bar with bacon in it? Some people even eat sandwiches made with chocolate and cheese. And the famous chili often served over spaghetti in Cincinnati, Ohio, commonly has a secret ingredient—cocoa!

Tasty Tidbits

The cocoa bean is used for more than just food. Cocoa butter is often used to heal dry skin and chapped lips.

Chocolate Barbeque Sauce

makes 4 servings

Ingredients:

2 tablespoons olive oil
1 onion, diced
4 large garlic cloves, chopped
2 tablespoons chili powder
1 tablespoon cumin
1 teaspoon coriander
¼ teaspoon cinnamon
1 tablespoon unsweetened cocoa powder
1 cup plain tomato sauce
½ cup brown sugar
1 cup brewed decaf coffee (or 1 tablespoon instant decaf coffee and 1 cup water)
½ cup red wine vinegar
2 tablespoons Worcestershire sauce
¼ cup molasses
1 tablespoon yellow mustard
salt and pepper

Directions:

1. Heat the olive oil in a medium pan on the stove top. Add the onion and garlic, and coat them with the hot oil. Stir until the onions are soft.
2. Stir in the chili powder, cumin, coriander, cinnamon, and cocoa, and cook for about 1 minute.
3. Add the tomato sauce and brown sugar. Cook, stirring until fully combined, about 2 minutes.
4. Stir in the decaf coffee, vinegar, Worcestershire sauce, molasses, and mustard.
5. Keep the stove top on low for about 25 minutes until the sauce thickens. Stir occasionally.
6. Allow the sauce to cool. Use immediately or cover and store in the fridge.

Cocoa goes well with meats such as beef and pork. Use this tasty barbeque sauce on pulled pork sandwiches!

Look for Fair Trade

Some cocoa is "fair trade." This means the cocoa bean farmers have been paid fairly for their crops, and those who worked on the product were treated well and paid enough.

Fair trade practices let farmers and cocoa processors use the best, local methods for making cocoa. Many people think fair trade chocolate tastes better because of this! When buying chocolate, look for the Fair Trade Certified™ label. As you're considering the health benefits of cocoa, thinking about the health of others and the world around you is a good idea too.

Tasty Tidbits

Each year, 35 million pounds (15,875 mt) of Fair Trade Certified cocoa are brought into the United States from countries such as the Ivory Coast, Peru, Dominican Republic, and Ecuador.

Why Eat Cocoa?

Cocoa Makes You Feel Good

- Eating cocoa has been shown to cause the brain to make the substances that boost mood and happiness.

Cocoa Is Heart Healthy

- The antioxidants in cocoa—flavanols—are said to lower blood pressure and improve blood flow to the brain and heart.

Cocoa Fills You Up

- The healthy fat in cocoa has lots of benefits, including helping us feel full longer. This can stop us from eating too much junk food!

Cocoa Boosts Energy

- Cocoa contains caffeine, which helps you feel energized and awake to run and play.

Glossary

allergy: a body's sensitivity to usually harmless things in the surroundings, such as dust, pollen, or mold

antioxidant: a substance that helps the body repair itself

cuisine: a style of cooking

equator: an imaginary line around Earth that is the same distance from the North and the South Poles

fat: one of the basic nutrients that supply energy to the body

ferment: to change a sugar or starch into an alcohol or acid in the absence of oxygen

ingredient: a food that is mixed with other foods

nutritional value: the makeup of a food and its impact on the body

process: to move something forward in a set of steps. Also, the set of steps itself.

recipe: an explanation of how to make a food

savory: full of flavor and spices, but not sweet

Fact Check

1. Cocoa beans come from __________.
   a. cocoa trees   b. cacao trees   c. chocolate trees

2. Which type of chocolate has the most health benefits?
   a. white chocolate   b. milk chocolate   c. dark chocolate

3. When was milk chocolate invented?
   a. 1500s   b. 1700s   c. 1876

Answers: 1. b, 2. c, 3. c

On the Internet

Healthy Chocolate Desserts to Cook with Kids
https://happykidskitchen.com/healthy-chocolate-desserts-to-cook-with-kids/
Get creative in the kitchen and check out healthy recipes that include—you guessed it—chocolate!

The Secret History of Chocolate
https://kids.nationalgeographic.com/history/article/the-secret-history-of-chocolate
This National Geographic Kids article takes readers through thousands of years of everyone's favorite treat.

Publisher's note to educators and parents: Our editors have carefully reviewed these websites to ensure that they are suitable for students. Many websites change frequently, however, and we cannot guarantee that a site's future contents will continue to meet our high standards of quality and educational value. Be advised that students should be closely supervised whenever they access the Internet.

Index